# THE TONY HART
# ART FACTORY · 2

**KAYE & WARD · LONDON**

# Introduction

This book, the second in the series of four, is mostly a 'doing things with paper' sort of book, plus a few exciting ideas for paper, wood and polystyrene sculpture. The use to which you can put paper, crayons, inks and paints is never ending. There are so many ways of using wax crayons, for example. Some of them you may never have come across before. You can make your own transfers in an unusual way and draw 'magic' pictures that appear in seconds.

You've probably done marbling patterns with oil paint and water, but I've discovered a new method that I think you'll find exciting. The various effects that are brought about by water are worth watching; for they can give you ideas for designs, pictures and patterns. Watch sun light on water – half shut your eyes and watch. Look at the patterns on the bottom of the swimming pool made by the light and moving water. What happens when there's oil on water? And see how water can change the pattern of sand or mud in stream beds or even in a gutter.

As for ink and paint, they can be made to do hundreds of exciting things. Paper can be used to make pictures just by cutting and folding it. Folded paper brings about shadows. What you see is a series of dark and light forms although you haven't marked the paper at all with ink or paint or anything! Because it's necessary to stick paper sometimes, I've included a bit about glues and paste and suggested the best for paper and the best for wood, plastic or anything else for which you need an adhesive. So – get stuck into it!

# Ink, wax and paper

# Marbling patterns

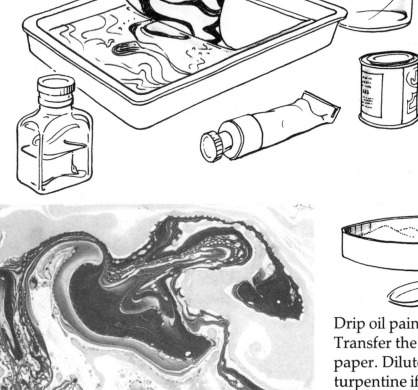

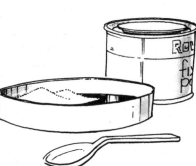

Drip oil paint onto clean water. Transfer the resulting pattern onto paper. Dilute the oil paint with turpentine if necessary. You can make your own oil paint by mixing powder colour with turpentine and thin oil.

Use cellulose paint from an aerosol spray on water to get these results. Work quickly or the cellulose becomes skin-like. Make sure the room is well ventilated as the fumes are not good for you.

Use your marbling patterns for collages.
Some patterns are particularly suitable
for sea, cloud or landscapes. Add detail
with pen or brush if it seems worth while.

You can mask the paper with
cut-out shapes *before*
transferring a marbling
pattern. It's best to use an
adhesive that can be peeled
off, like Spraymount or
Latex.

Mix wallpaper paste in a flat dish.
2 teaspoons to 1 pint of water.

Draw stick backwards and
forwards across surface.

Drip oil paint onto surface.

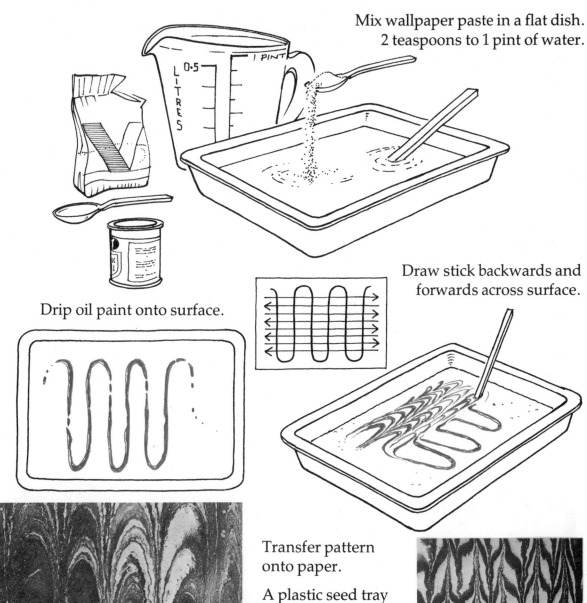

Transfer pattern
onto paper.

A plastic seed tray
makes a good dish.
Some patterns make
good backgrounds
for drawings and
paintings.

Experiment with
two colours and
thinner or thicker
paint.

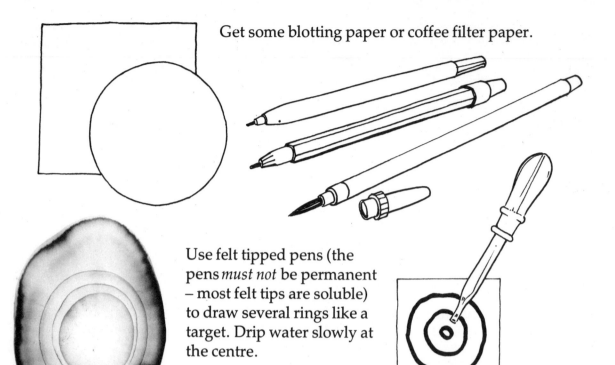

Get some blotting paper or coffee filter paper.

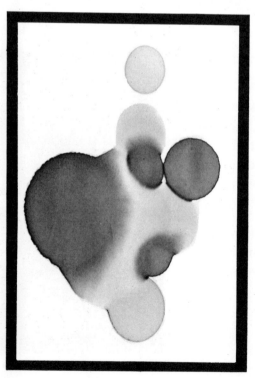

Use felt tipped pens (the pens *must not* be permanent – most felt tips are soluble) to draw several rings like a target. Drip water slowly at the centre.

Draw simple shapes on blotting paper. Lay on water for 2 seconds. Tear or cut blotting paper up and form a collage. This can be done wet or dry.

Ink and water dripped onto blotting paper.

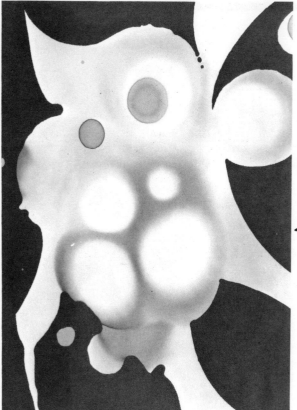

Oil or candle grease dripped onto blotting paper will resist ink or water colour. Candle grease can then be cracked off when completely dry.

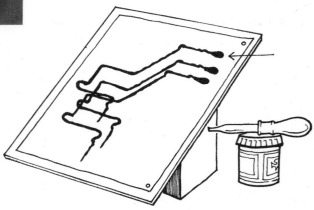

An ink run pattern is made by putting a few drops of ink onto a sheet of card and tilting and moving the card. An unusual repeat pattern is made by putting several drops down and then tilting and rotating.

Rub damp cotton wool onto card or paper leaving dry areas. Ink is then touched lightly to the wet areas. The handle end of a brush can be used for the inking. If the ink does not spread quickly, add one drop of washing-up liquid to the ink bottle.

Prints from card tubes and edges on wet and dry paper.

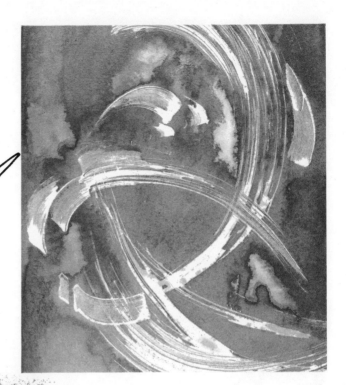

Brush Latex adhesive in a few bold strokes over white card. When this Latex is dry (½ hour) brush over with ink – any sort. When this is dry, rub off the Latex.

Stick paper strips temporarily to a background and over-paint with paint, ink or crayon. So that the masking strips can be removed easily, stick them with Spraymount (a temporary mounting adhesive) or small dots of Latex adhesive.

A drop of paint can be blown to form tree- and root-like shapes. Use a plastic straw for blowing.

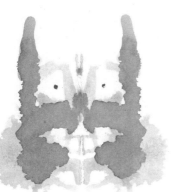

Blot patterns without a fold. Use thick poster paint on a sheet of polythene. Fold and press the paint into shape. Open. Transfer onto a sheet of paper.

Tissue paper, folded twice. Fold leaving *overlaps* (so you can unfold it easily later).

Brush a little water onto the folded tissue. Brush ink and dab onto paper. Unfold carefully.

Cut tissue and ink on damp paper.

Oriental brush and ink stick.
Lamp black can be used instead.
Hold brush upright and move
whole arm.

White chalk
rubbed onto grey
card. Brush
strokes in lamp
black.

Cat painted with
clear water.
Chinese ink
applied with
edge of brush.

Paint design with water. It is best to paint a little at a time. Touch ink to wet area.

Experiment with two colours within the same area. See colour picture on Page **2**.15

Black and diluted ink. Paint slowly and *continuously*. Don't stop when painting a form or you'll get tide marks!

For sharp lines, let one feature dry before painting another over it. The spots on the dark pig were made by allowing drops of water to fall on the dried ink and then blotting them with blotting paper.

Rub candle wax to and fro over white card. Apply ink with cotton wool.

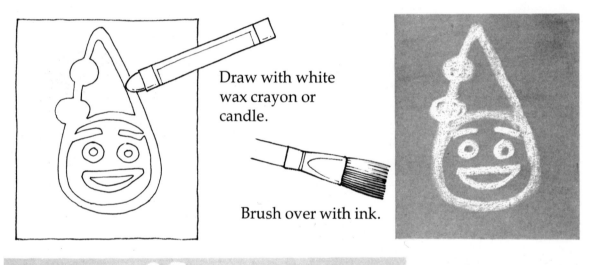

Draw with white wax crayon or candle.

Brush over with ink.

When one coat of ink has dried you can ink over again in selected places.

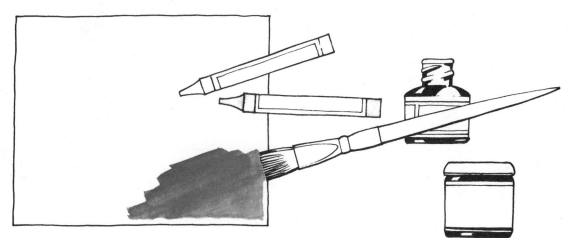

## Wax scraper-board

Scribble with light-coloured wax crayon onto white card. Paint all over with black indian ink. The ink covers more easily if you add a little black poster paint.

When dry, scrape your design, using sharpened edges of blocks of wood or a wood stylus.

## Wax transfer

Cover white paper with
white chalk – rub in well with finger. Over that, draw wax crayon lines.
Use two or more colours. Reverse paper onto a blank sheet of white or coloured
paper and draw a picture or pattern using wooden stylus or pencil.

Card tilt pattern. Poster paint and water.
Blown paint, using drinking straw.

Water design with
dripped ink.

Pig pattern. Soluble ink.

Chinese brushes
and ink for
oriental art
forms.

Poster paint.
Butterfly fold blot.

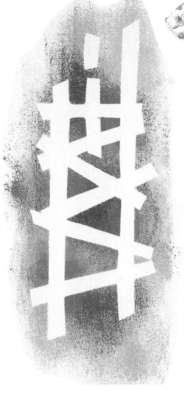

Poster paint
and stencil
brush over
masking
strips.

Chinese brush
and ink on
damp card.

Wax and ink scraper board
design.

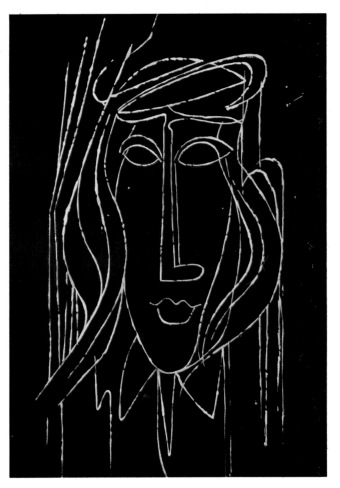

Wax crayon and chalk
transfer.

Tissue paper and ink
fold pattern.

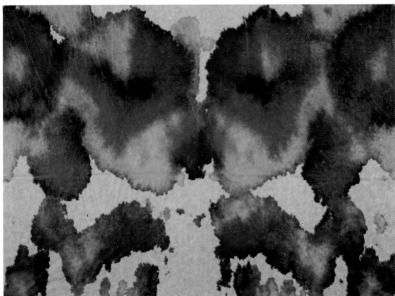

Card fold creatures. Light card and felt tip pens.

Paper straws. Cutting, pressing and bending.

### Transferring newsprint

Cut pictures, lettering or words from newspaper. Rub candle wax over newsprint. Reverse onto plain paper and rub with thumb-nail or bowl of spoon.

Make an impression into thick cardboard using a wood stylus. It should be at least 1 mm deep. Place a sheet of thin paper over the top and rub with wax candle or crayon. Now brush ink over the rubbed wax.

**Molten wax pictures.** (When someone grown up is ironing!) Scrape tiny pieces of wax crayon onto a piece of paper that has been folded and opened. Use 2 or 3 colours. Refold. Ask mother to iron the folded paper. Put lots of newspaper underneath and a piece between the iron and the folded paper.

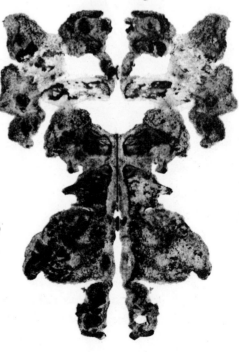

Ask your mother to iron a piece of card for you so it is warm. Draw on it with wax crayons.

# PAPER

Cut tissue paper can be overlapped to produce different tones. It's easier to cut if you fold it between ordinary paper. Clear gum or wallpaper paste is best to stick it down.

Overlapping different colours of tissue is effective.

Different weights of paper can be cut into shapes and stuck down to make a collage.

Some magazine illustrations lend themselves to particular picture forms.

A surrealist picture. The pieces were put together from cut out magazine illustrations.

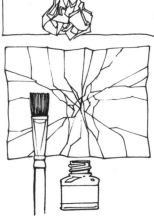

Score or fold card to give it a different texture. Crumple paper and unfold, brush ink over it, then wipe off the surplus ink. Try using these together with matt and gloss paper in a collage.

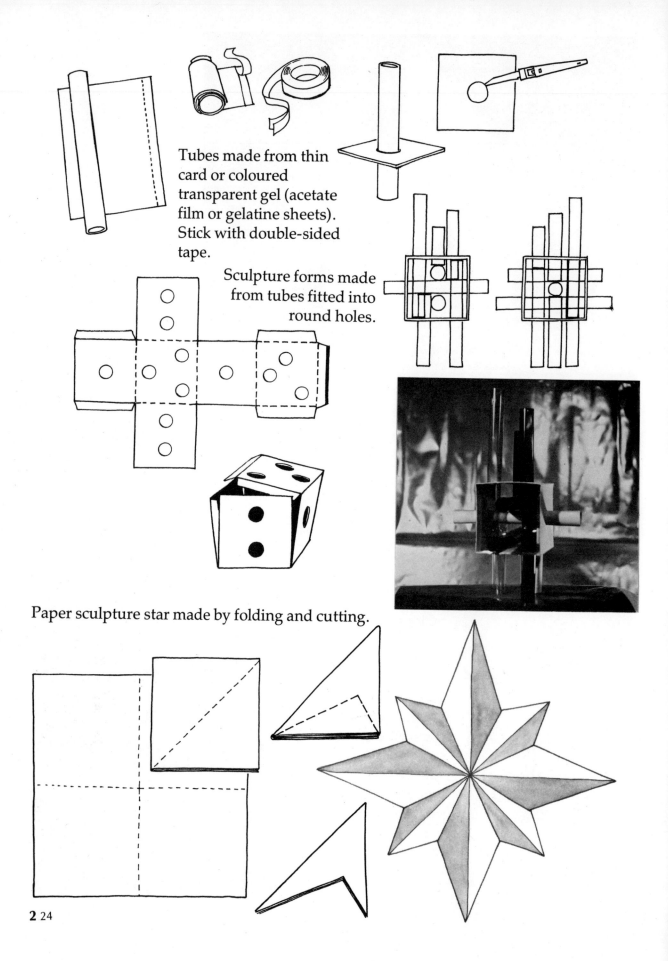

Tubes made from thin card or coloured transparent gel (acetate film or gelatine sheets). Stick with double-sided tape.

Sculpture forms made from tubes fitted into round holes.

Paper sculpture star made by folding and cutting.

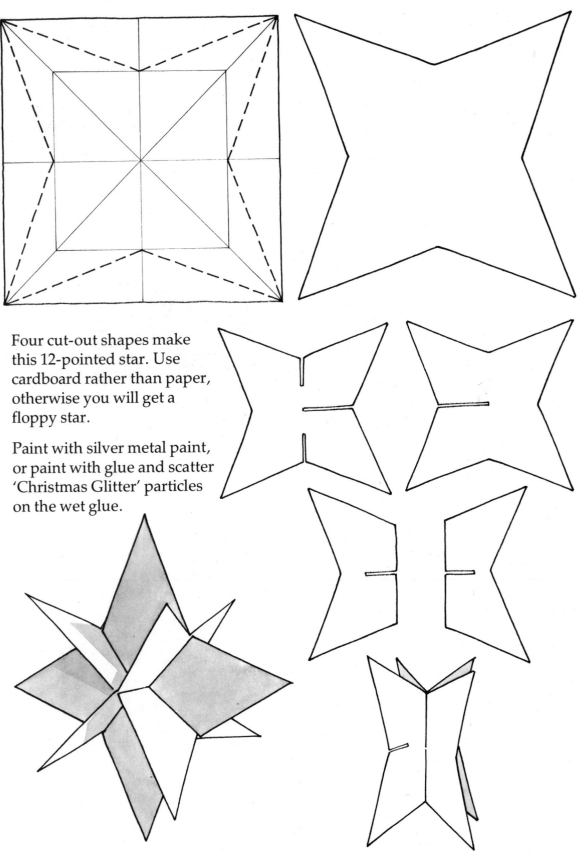

Four cut-out shapes make this 12-pointed star. Use cardboard rather than paper, otherwise you will get a floppy star.

Paint with silver metal paint, or paint with glue and scatter 'Christmas Glitter' particles on the wet glue.

**Paper animals.** Make a cardboard template and use to draw both sides of the creature. Use cartridge paper or thin card for these. Paint with poster paint or use felt tip colours. See colour picture on page **2**.18.

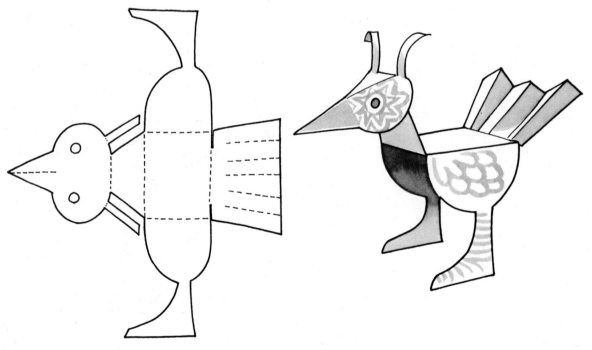

This sort of paper sculpture needs good quality cartridge paper. Use a sharp craft knife for cutting and scoring. If anything needs to be stuck down, use small spots of Latex adhesive. The paper sculpture should be mounted on coloured card to set it off. Never paint the cartridge paper. The interest is in the crisp paper forms and the shadows resulting from the relief forms.

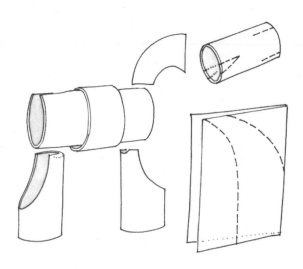

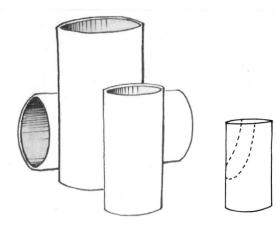

Toilet roll centres or cardboard tubes are used to make the body, legs and head of this horse; thin card for the neck and tail.

Free-standing forms are made by slotting the two cut-out pieces together.

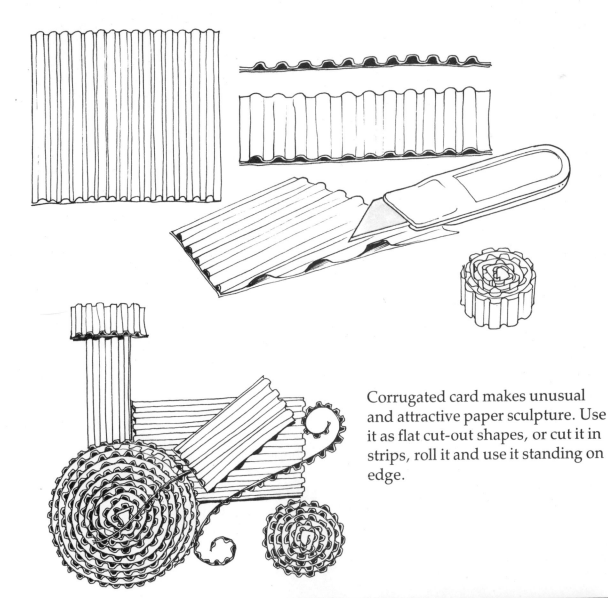

Corrugated card makes unusual and attractive paper sculpture. Use it as flat cut-out shapes, or cut it in strips, roll it and use it standing on edge.

When cutting use a craft knife or scissors. The angle at which you cut corrugated card makes a difference to the pattern of the edge.

The craft knife should be sharp, otherwise the cut edge of the corrugated card will fray and look messy. But be careful not to cut your fingers, or ask an adult to do the cutting for you.

## Art straws

Paper straws – not plastic – can be cut, stuck and tied to make unlimited shapes and patterns. If you are colouring the straws it's best to paint a lot of them with different-coloured poster paint before they are cut.

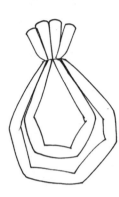

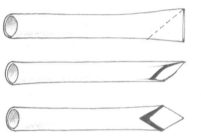

## Wood sculpture
(free standing)

With a tenon saw, sandpaper and a supply of wood off-cuts you can create the most satisfying constructions. You will find that many scrap pieces of wood need nothing more than sandpapering. Others you may wish to cut to a different shape. Wood stains are obtainable for colouring. A tube of impact adhesive will do all the sticking necessary.

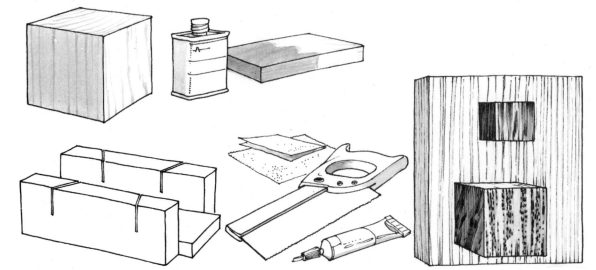

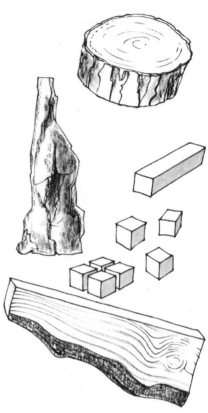

## Wood sculpture (Wall plaque)

Choose a wooden baseboard with an interesting grain. It is cheaper to use a wood laminate. Find pieces of wood with differing textures: bark, log sections and small pieces cut from wood dowling. It's the placing of the pieces that makes the picture. Don't stick them down until you are satisfied.
Wood bark and timber form a landscape with pressed leaves forming a treescape.

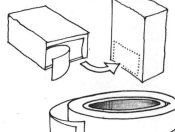

Polystyrene is useful for all sorts of shapes and forms. Carefully cut with a craft knife or saw it with a bread knife, or mark out your pattern and get an adult to do the cutting for you. You can buy an electric hot wire which cuts by melting the plastic.

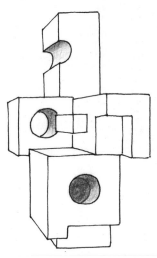

Polystyrene packing often looks like modern sculpture. If sticking polystyrene use a multi-purpose adhesive that will not melt the polystyrene.

For Wood, use a clear, quick-drying modelling cement for sticking, or double-sided sticky tape.

## Polystyrene plaque

Polystyrene ceiling tiles and off-cuts are used to put together this lightweight wall plaque. It is important to use a light, sharp craft knife to cut polystyrene otherwise you will get a crumbly edge. Ask an adult to do the cutting for you. Many adhesives melt the plastic so use a universal adhesive to do the sticking.

First published by Kaye & Ward Ltd
Century House, 82/84 Tanner Street, London SE1 3PP
1980

ISBN 0 7182 1264 9

Typeset by John Smith, London
Printed in Hong Kong by Everbest Printing Co., Ltd.